Across the sea

Daryl Johnson Jr.

BookLeaf
Publishing

India | USA | UK

Presentation by *BookLeaf Publishing*

Web: www.bookleafpub.com

E-mail: info@bookleafpub.com

ISBN: 9789357445740

First edition 2022

For my grandmother, Bonnie Johnson.
We did it, grandma, I hope I'm making you
proud from the clouds
I love you.

Night shift

Rolling up to work on my brand new bike
someone stole my last one, this one's small like
old trike
But no matter cause I'm only here to work five
to nine
Pray to God that it's not busy, pray I get off on
time

Walk through the door, already I start to mourn
Cause I'm looking at my coworkers, I thought
there'd be more
Turns out Jill called in sick, said she'd be back in
the morn
But her snap story proves she's the biggest liar
ever born

Really not that surprised, nevertheless I'm pissed
still
And it turns out three drivers quit, we lost Kate,
Mark and Bill
Ah yes, I guess, once again understaffed
Ah yes, I guess, tonight's gonna kick my ass

Get clocked in, bring in my bike from outside

Send a text to the rents, hide from cameras off to
the side
Cute coworker says hi so I reply with a blush
Then I take my place at the front counter and
wait for dinner rush

Two seconds later, a blank fires, now we're off
Already have a bad customer, he's pissed and he
scoffs
"I didn't order that," Sir I read it all back to you
I got the whole order right, what the fuck do you
want me to do

And somebody pick up that goddamn phone,
do I have to run this whole place on my own
Fuck this shit, I don't get enough money for this
shit
Fuck this shit, fuck this shit, motherfucking
night shift

Scheduled out at nine, now it's nine past eleven
Somehow all the other insiders got out around
seven
I'm the last worker and it's ball busting busy
And there's so many dicks up in the lobby, man I
feel just like Lizzy

Caplan while coping with music, standing and
hoping
For closing time to come and bust and get here
faster cause fuck
I'm out of fucks to give, like all of us, we're shit
out of luck
Cause here, we're stuck chasing just above that
minimum buck

Ford friends

I must admit
your friendship's forfeit bore a hole
in my chest-chambers
gaping wounds that allow my blood
to spill as coagulated oil for organic pistons
out unto the driveway pavement
I'm an old Ford, you, my whisked away V8
engine
both of little use separated.

I am rusting in Cupid's garage
while you give some other metal steed drive
I rust, yet love still.

I hope you rust, too.

Diagnosis

Doctor's appointment
sweaty palms, weak knees, red face
diagnosis: her

In dreams

She haunts me in my dreams
I am not strong enough to exorcise her
some nights she wears a beautiful wedding dress
slow dancing in the moonlight to the tempo of
our hearts
other nights she's asleep in my arms
after a night of passion under the pale moonlight
and I am happy

then she vanishes, and I am alone once more
I can't have her
I can't get rid of her
but she's once more mine in dreams

or are they nightmares?

Ego

Hello everybody, my name is Daryl Johnson
I was told we're reading poems, they're not great,
but I've got some
The things I write are odd, they seem kind of
obscure
Also I don't swear, but please, my poems aren't
manure
I don't think much of myself, so please don't be
mean
I hope you like my poems, even though they
don't much gleam
Don't worry, my time up here won't be very long
And without further ado, here's my story, here's
my song.

Good evening, I'm Daryl Johnson, how do you
do?
Thank you all for coming out, we've got quite
the show for you
Here on Open Mic Night, this is where I shine
best

Don't worry, I'm not an amateur, so put all your
fears to rest
I've got some pretty good poems, some are
happy, others, sad
We've got a pretty good lineup, so stick around,
you'll be glad
Now I'll kick things off, I come hard with bars
and rhymes
I may not be the best, but I know I'm gonna give
you all a good time.

WOO-HOO! GOOD EVENING OPEN MIC
NIGHT
PUT YOUR SUNGLASSES ON, I'VE HEARD
MY SWAGGER SHINES BRIGHT
I'M HERE TO STEAL THIS WIN AND ADD
IT TO MY GROWING LIST OF DUBS
CAUSE I'M A GOD WITH THE MIC, I'LL
OUTPERFORM THESE OTHER BUBS
MY NAME IS DARYL MOTHERFUCKING
JOHNSON, I DON'T HAVE AN EQUAL
I WIN BATTLE AFTER BATTLE EVERY
TIME LIKE THE SEQUEL
I'M THE ALPHA OF THIS COMPETITION,
I'M A FUCKING EAGLE

ALL THESE OTHER POETS CAN FIGHT
FOR MY SCRAPS CAUSE THEY'RE
SEAGULLS

Junior

We share a name and we share a face
Live together and in college, in life, the same
place
Sometimes I hold our name high and with pride
But while things cruise on for you, my drive's a
bumpy ride

When you spite me, you take my dignity and I
feel small
When you strike me, you stand over me so you
feel tall
You only like me when I sacrifice my happiness
for yours
You only like me when I'm a quiet mess or doing
chores

When you're around, my heart drops down into
my chest
Then you pet me and you vet me until I have no
secrets left
Don't say you only want what's best while you're
pounding on your chest
You only love what you control, like
Jekyll/Hyde in a sense

Most days I can't stand looking like you
Because you're everything I fear, I don't want to
be anything like you
I want to cut my face off, remove the features
like a tumor
Because I'm not even my own person, I'm your
Junior.

I'm not even my own person
I'm just a Junior.

Dear Mr. President

Dear Mr. President
I turn eighteen soon
I'm a young U.S resident
youth is my one boon
I love my home a lot
there's nothing else like it
our peoples are diverse
our providences united
I'm starting a new chapter
cause I'll be eighteen soon
but I don't want to go overseas
please don't send me to my doom
my mother raised a poet
not a soldier, but her joy
never want to shoulder muskets
to kill someone else's boy
Please don't draft me, spare my life
I have other things to give
Mr. President, I'm begging you
please just let me live.

Breakup

Where does the love go
when you break up with someone?
Was it ever real?

Masterpiece

When I look at you
something pops into my head
one word: masterpiece.

Life without liberty

Life without liberty
Is a life filled with tyranny
For a sad sack like me
Everyone lacks sympathy

Life without liberty
Is a life lived indifferently
Vicious dogs led by wicked hogs
Eat young activists who act timidly

Life without liberty
Obviously means sympathy
Very well might go extinct unless
Everyone acts differently.

Heaven

A question for God
when I make it to Heaven
will it be worth it?

Never really here

After our last argument
I knew our end was near
But oh my dear, I seem to fear
That you were never really here.

Across the sea

Across the sea in front of me
awaits an unknown destiny
but this I know, it compels me so
to seek out lands that I don't know
to venture places far and wide
to better learn myself inside
unsure of things that lie in wait
but certain there I'll meet my fate.

Across the sea in front of me
I might find friend or enemy
someone with which to share my life
or be met with hate and endless strife?
will I find grief and pain alone
or find a place that I'll call home?
if I leave now, will I be missed
or be courted and met with Hades' kiss?

Across the sea in front of me
has always been a mystery

a question within, one of woe
should I stay or should I go?
I stand alone on friendly sand
on the very edge of my homeland
torn between the sea and pier
should I sail away or stay right here?

Before the sand that outlines my land
lies the place where I became a man
I know these trees, I know these lands.
I know this place like the back of my hand
I know the town, I know the roads
I know the ground, I know the folks
I've known a life that's hard and sweet
but I also know it's not complete.

My body is young, my mind too spry
to be bested by life and let life pass by
so I step on the boat, anxious with glee
to begin my journey across the sea.

Across the sea in front of me
awaits an unknown destiny
I'll be gone a while, but don't miss me
I hope to see you across the sea.

My destiny lies in front of me
my destiny lies across the sea.

Talking to myself in the dark

My room is dark and quiet
it's half past midnight and I'm too tired to sleep
I beg for Him to help me
to show me the light
but nothing comes
I pray for sweet dreams, for dreams at all
the nightmares have been getting too real lately
I fear falling asleep and falling victim to the
monsters that find me in my dreams
They tell you the beasts hide under your bed
they fail to tell you about the ones in your head
Please, make it stop
Father, if you're there
Please, a sign
Please.

I need to stop talking to myself in the dark
only fools do that.

Someone

I've tried to pursue
so many girls since her, yet
I still miss someone.

Between her legs

I wonder who's between her legs
I like to think that I've moved on from her
but on nights I long for her to be mine again
my mind can't help but wonder
is he taller? Does he have a six pack under his
shirt?
is his skin darker than mine, like rich Belgium
chocolate
or is it lighter, more like freshly fallen snow?
I doubt his hair gets messy like mine, or maybe
it does and she doesn't mind
arc his eyes brown like mine, or something
different? Blue? Hazel?
Different from mine, I'm sure.

I wonder, does who she have between her legs
love her as much as I did?
Does he want to share the rest of his days with
her
and give her children?

Or is she just a trophy to him, another conquest
in his eyes
another notch under his belt?
Does he make her laugh, smile throughout the
day?
Does he remind her how beautiful she is
as much as I did?
I hope he treats her right.

I remember her loving indiscriminately
maybe she traded me for more feminine
company
Would it be worst if she left me for a girl, or a
boy?
I'm not sure if I'll ever be able to answer that
question
or any of the other ones she left me with
except for one
if she can love and lust for all of the billions
of people on Earth, then the possibilities are
endless
I may never know who's between her legs
but I know who isn't.

What We Call The End

Over a century ago, we used words on a regular basis
That were associated with What We Called the End;
Trench warfare, mustard gas, artillery, machine guns, tanks, bombers, airships,
No Man's Land.
That last one is technically a lie, for if land does not belong to Man
Why has so much of Man's blood been shed on it?
For every yard gained from each skirmish lies a dead man, with the yards numbering the thousands
Yet we call it No Man's Land?
The dead beg to differ, and to call it No Man's Land

They say, "This land? That seems to belong not
to Man? This is our land
For we have given all that we are for this plain
This vast earthy sea, devoid of life and beauty
that stretches between our trenches is ours
For our lives were given and our blood was shed
For King and Country, for Tsar, Kaiser and
Sultan, but also for our families,
So you can't say this land belongs to no Man
For we've lived and died to purchase this land
And it does not matter how Death found us;
By gas or grenade, by bullet or bombardment
He found us, and it does not matter where Death
found us;
 Verdun, Gallipoli, the Somme or the Marne,
The River Meuse, the Argonne Forest, The Suez
Canal or Passchendaele
He found us, and for everywhere we perished,
sits the land we bought with our bodies."

The Hells these men experienced was dubbed
The War to End All Wars
And the weapons, forged of steel, made by man,
turned the Heavens upside down
Letting ash and hellfire rain down from the
depths of the Underworld
In a catalyst the world believed to be
Armageddon.

Yet now, over a century later, we have forgotten
such a war
And it seems our world leaders are ready for
another apocalypse
And this one won't be called "The War to End
All Wars"
But rather, "The War to End All Life"
Well, maybe not
Who will be left to call it that?
What would survive to Name our End?
Nothing, afterwards
But before it comes, maybe we can
If we're quick enough.

Today, just a century after peace temporarily
controlled the world
We have new words to describe What We Call
the End;
Nuclear, Hidden Agendas, Twitter, War Pigs, red
buttons
Democracy, Communism, bigotry, drones
Corruption, murder, tyranny
Missile tests, missile launches, military
conscription, defense spending
The contest to see what country can outgun the
other,
Mutually Assured Destruction
Any Day Now.

All of these words can be used to describe
What Will Be Our End
But only before, never after
Because this time, if the World goes to War
There will be no armistice to save us
For there will be nothing left to save
And it's happening soon, in our near future. I can
see it now.
Our leaders growing tired of pointless
diplomacy, the guns being manufactured
By the thousands,
Brave men and women, good men and women
everywhere
Dying in fields, trenches and destroyed cities
As thousands of younger men and women,
Boys and Girls, are conscripted into the War
As the draft resembling that of the Vietnam
Conflict is reinstated
And our fresh troops will be sent overseas,
Where they will become fresh meat
And where they will only be sent back in
Black boxes or black bags.
The War will be televised,
It will at times, be live
And the world will cry, but not stop
It will mourn, but not yield
And we will all butcher each other like cattle,
until What We Call the End

Has passed
And by the time we, on both sides of the war,
remember that the Old Lie
Is still an Old Lie,
It will be too late.
For Death will find us. He always does
And the dead from so many years ago will see
us rip each other's throats out
And bleed unto the Earth as they did,
And they will shake their heads in
Disappointment and pity,
But they will stay silent.
And after the bombs are dropped
And the ash clears away
To reveal the charred corpses of All of Earth's
peoples,
Only then will the dead speak
And all they will say is,
"Now it is No Man's Land."

Wi-Fi

The Wi-Fi went out
no Youtube or anime
just me and my thoughts

Moonlight

My dreams consist of dances
the waltz, the swing, the tango
with maidens donning ball gowns and dresses
flowing freely in the pale moonlight
the shy goddess, our only on-looker.

mirrored images compete for my affections
unknowingly and unwillingly
as if I were Zeus, love gon to Io and Callisto
who will dance with me?

could it be the love demon
or will Persephone decide to participate
after May's long depression?

who takes my hand in the moonlight
in the pale, in the crimson?

I can't dance
who will learn to dance with me?

My outreached hands await
who will dance with me?
Who?

To my Lieutenant

To my Lieutenant,
my best friend, my right hand
we've had quite the adventure
and you were my best man.

We've had our fun, but now I need to rest
you'll need to be strong if you're to survive what
comes next
it's time for me to leave, my father calls me
home
so you're gonna have to carry on with your
journey alone.

Remember your manners, always be polite
never lash out against a loved one in spite
tell people that you love them, even if it's hard
and never give up on your dreams, never fold
your cards.

My friend, please take care of my kids and my
wife

do what makes you happy, let regret never fill
your life
please me confident and brave, don't let fear
become a tenant
I love you, my friend, I have faith in you,
Lieutenant.

You were always there for me, I wish I had time
to repay you
you were always in my heart, please believe in
what I say to you
smart and intelligent, kind and strong-willed
and I pray you destroy all those that mean you
ill.

I leave you in good faith that you'll tend to my
affairs
that you'll get them all in order and handle them
with care
I love you, my friend, but my end is now
eminent
thank you for your service and your love, my
Lieutenant.

Life Shift

Damn, waited so long, never thought I'd make it
to this stage
I've come of age, now I make pizzas, chasing
minimum wage
I'm an adult now, a man, but damn, is this it?
After all the stress and obstacles, I thought that
it'd be different
Working on this night shift, really got me in my
head
Despite past things I've said, I'd rather be living
than dead
But how come I'm doing everything that I
should be in life
I was happy younger, now every day's filled
with strife
I was told that I'd be happy, seems I was
misinformed
Because I feel older than my age, my soul's
stuck in the wrong form
Wasn't ready for the world, this new sense of
adulting

I'm terrified of these responsibilities I'm
confronting
I'm having a life shift.

Who do I go to if I have an issue that applies to
me?
Please be honest, it seems as though everybody
lies to me
Is everybody unhappy or is it just me?
Am I overreacting or do I just some more sleep
When disrespected, how come I have to be the
bigger man?
Just today on the phone, got called something
sounding like rigger, damn
You think I like stressing over college and
slinging pizza after hours
Dude I'm no different than most teenagers, just
want to get ours
Burying past selves and relationships, I guess
Sayonara
All this trial tribulations got me weeping like
Llorona
Thought that after doing everything I should be
doing this stage
I'd feel good about myself, but all I feel's grief
and rage
In the middle of a life shift.

Look son, you're an adult, you've finally grown
into a man
And I'm gonna to everything about the world
that I can
Go to college, go and get a good degree
If you do that, I don't care about your major, I'll
agree
Now one day soon, you'll start your life not
knowing what do you
But essentially being an adult means doing shit
you don't wanna do
Like working near death shifts at a low paying
job you hate
Sacrifice all your time and money for some girl
you want to date
And if that bitch breaks your heart, on to the
next
Never settle for less, never give up until you're
the best
And when you bury me, the grief feels like the
Earth on your shoulders
Because life is just a punishment, reach the top
with that boulder
Just like Sisyphus
I'm having a life shift.

Acknowledgements

I wish to thank many people for my journey to getting published; first to BookLeaf Publishing for even considering helping me, none of this would have happened in the first place; to my wonderful mother, father and brother, for always pushing me to pursue my dreams of writing; to my Lieutenant, they know who they are, thank you for all of your love and loyalty to me over the years; to my amazing friends, whom I lovingly refer to as "the bois," you are all the best brothers I could have ever hoped to have, I love you all; and most of all, to my grandmother, for everything she's done for me and my family over the years. I love you and hope I can be everything you said I could be over the years. Thank you all from the bottom of my heart and here's to hopefully many more books to come.